FINE GRAINED OUTSOURCED DATA PUNCTURING IN CLOUD

P. Abinaya, J. Senthil Kumar, R. Padhmapriya, K. Prathiksha

Mepco Schlenk Engineering College (Autonomous), Sivakasi

ABSTRACT

Cloud storage is one of the most appealing features of cloud computing. The shared data in cloud servers, however, usually contains users' sensitive information (e.g., personal profile, financial data, health records, etc.) and needs to be well protected. For the users those who are using cloud computing, the major problem that arises is the disclose of the data that are very sensitive. The assured data deletion of cloud based on cryptography mainly focuses on enhancement and strengthening process of Third-party key accessing. The main idea here is that the data of any format is encrypted and then outsourced to the cloud, wherein the type of the data is identified before deletion is performed. Then at last permanent deletion is done for the data that has to be deleted permanently by the data owner. The attribute-based encryption generates the cipher text and each cipher text is defined by a set of tags. The data owners define a deletion policy to specify the cipher text to be deleted. It deletes the cipher which matches the puncture policy defined by the data owners. Once deleted, it cannot be decrypted using the secret key.

ACKNOWLEDGEMENT

First and foremost, we thank the **LORD ALMIGHTY** for his abundant blessings that is showered upon our past, present and future successful endeavors.

We extend our sincere gratitude to our college management and Principal **Dr. S. Arivazhagan M.E., Ph.D.,** for providing sufficient working environment such as systems and library facilities. We also thank him very much for providing us with adequate lab facilities, which enable us to complete out project.

We would like to extend our heartfelt gratitude to **Dr.J. Rajasekar**, M.E., Ph.D., Professor and Head, Department of Computer Science and Engineering, Mepco Schlenk Engineering College for giving me the golden opportunity to undertake a project of this nature and for his most valuable guidance given at every phase of our work.

We would also like to extend our gratitude to **Mr.B. Lakshmanan.,** Assistant Professor (Sr. Grade), Department of Computer Science and Engineering, Mepco Schlenk Engineering College for being our Project Coordinator and directing us throughout our project.

We would also like to extend our gratitude and sincere thanks to **Mrs. P. Abinaya**, M.E.,Assistant Professor (Sr. Grade), Department of Computer Science and Engineering, Mepco Schlenk Engineering College for being our Project Guide for her moral support and suggestions. She has put her valuable experience and expertise in directing, suggesting and supporting us throughout the Project to bring out the best.

Our Sincere thanks to our revered **faculty members and lab technicians** for their help over this project work.

Last but not least, we extend our indebtedness towards our beloved **family and our friends** for their support which made the project a successful one.

TABLE OF CONTENTS

CHAPTER NO.	TITLE	PAGE NO.

LIST OF ABBREVIATIONS

Abbreviation	Expansion
PK	Public Parameters
MK	Master Key
SK	Private Key
A	Attributes
CT	Cipher text
S	Set of Attributes

INTRODUCTION

CHAPTER 1

INTRODUCTION

1.1 PROJECT DESCRIPTION

As more and more services and applications are emerging in the Internet, exposing sensitive data in the Internet has become easier. The outsourced data are out of the Data Owners control. We also do not know how to securely delete the unneeded sensitive data stored in cloud to prevent potential data leakage issues is a big challenge. A self-controlled outsourced data expunge method in cloud-based IoT enables the Data Owners to precisely and permanently delete their outsourced IoT-driven data in a policy-based way without relying on the Cloud Server.

1.2 PURPOSE OF THE PROJECT

In recent years emerging technologies uses cloud for storing their public and private data. the data stored in cloud may be leaked or misused by some hackers without the knowledge of data owners. Data users can access the stored data whereas they cannot be deleted or decrypted without the knowledge of data owners. If data owners feel that the data has been unnecessary, they can delete their data. once deleted the outsourced encrypted data cannot be decrypted again.

1.3 OBJECTIVE OF THE PROJECT

Main objective of the proposed work is,

- To upload a needed file or document to the cloud.
- To encrypt the file that seems to be confidential.
- To decrypt the data for viewing whenever needed.
- To delete the data permanently from the cloud if the data owners feel it to be unnecessary so that it can't be retrieved anywhere from the cloud.

1.4 OUTCOMES OF THE PROJECT

The outcomes of the proposed work are,

- The file to be processed is outsourced to the cloud.
- The outsourced data is then converted into cipher text (unreadable by human).
- The original file can be viewed in human readable format.
- The outsourced encrypted sensitive data should be expunged from the cloud permanently.

1.5 SUMMARY

This chapter had given the brief description about the purpose of the project, objectives, outcomes and organization of the report.

LITERATURE SURVEY

CHAPTER 2
LITERATURE SURVEY

2.1 OVERVIEW

Here in this paper the methodologies were discussed from previous works for our proposed system.

2.2 Secure and Fine-Grained Self-Controlled Outsourced Data Deletion in Cloud Based IoT

Author name: JIALU HAO, STUDENT MEMBER, IEEE, JIAN LIU, WEI WU, FENGYI TANG, AND MING XIAN

Year: 2020

Given that outsourced data is out of DOs physical control and the cloud server (CS) cannot always be fully trusted, securing the deletion of unwanted sensitive data stored in the cloud to prevent data leaking is a major difficulty. Most previous systems only offer coarse-grained deletion and rely on the CS's participation, severely limiting their flexibility and applicability. We present a secure and fine-grained self-controlled outsourced data deletion technique in cloud-based IoT in this research, based on an upgraded policy-based puncturable encryption (P-PUN-ENC) primitive. Our scheme's key contribution is that it allows DOs to remove their outsourced IoT-driven data precisely and permanently using a policy-based approach without relying on the CS. Then, in attribute-based encryption (ABE), we use a key delegation approach to finish the key update processes. In addition, we present the outsourced policy-based puncturable encryption (OP-PUN-ENC) primitive, which combines the key and decryption outsource technique with PPUN-ENC to address the issue of escalating key storage and decryption costs in P-PUN-ENC. Comprehensive comparisons reveal that our suggested scheme is more capable of meeting data deletion requirements in cloud-based IoT, and formal security proofs and extensive simulation results confirm the proposed scheme's dependability and efficiency.

2.3 CP-ABE-Based Secure and Verifiable Data Deletion in Cloud

Author name: JUN MA, MINSHEN WANG , JINBO XIONG AND YONGJIN HU.

Year: 2021

Because data from various smart mobile devices invariably contains personal information, cloud data, whose ownership is separated from their administration, frequently contain users' private information. This is especially true in the fifth-generation mobile communication (5G) environment. If information is not securely erased in a timely manner, or if the result of data deletion after its expiration cannot be verified, major difficulties such as unauthorised access and data privacy disclosure will arise. As a result, this has a negative impact on cloud data security and stymies the development of cloud computing services. To enable fine-grained secure data deletion and deletion verification for cloud data, we present a unique secure data deletion and verification (SDVC) scheme based on CP-ABE in this study. We build an attribute association tree based on the idea of access policy in CP-ABE to perform rapid revoking attribute and re encrypting key to accomplish fine-grained control of secure key deletion. We also create a rule transposition technique to generate random data blocks, and we combine overwriting technology with the Merkle hash tree to provide secure cypher text deletion and develop a validator, which is then used to verify the data deletion result. Through theoretical analysis and extensive simulation experiment findings, we validate the SDVC scheme's security under the standard model and verify its correctness and effectiveness.

2.4 Secure Cloud Storage with Data Dynamics Using Secure Network Coding Techniques

Author name: BINANDA SENGUPTA, AKANKSHA DIXIT, AND SUSHMITA RUJ, SENIOR MEMBER, IEEE

Year: 2020

Cloud users with limited storage might outsource their data to remote servers in the age of cloud computing. In exchange for monetary compensation, these servers guarantee the irretrievability of their clients' data at any moment. Clients can validate the integrity of outsourced data using secure cloud storage techniques. In this paper, we look into the feasibility of building a secure cloud storage system for dynamic data using secure network coding algorithms. We illustrate how several secure network coding schemes can be utilised to build efficient secure cloud storage protocols for dynamic data, and we build one (DSCS I) based on one. DSCS I is the first secure cloud storage protocol for dynamic data built utilising secure network coding techniques that is secure in the standard model, to the best of our knowledge. Although generic dynamic data allows for unrestricted insertions, deletions, and updates, append-only data has a wide range of real-world uses. We develop a new secure cloud storage protocol (DSCS II) for append-only data that overcomes some of the shortcomings of DSCS I. Finally, in order to evaluate the performance of DSCS I and DSCS II, we give prototype implementations.

2.5 A New Communication-Efficient Privacy-Preserving Range Query Scheme in Fog-Enhanced IoT

Author name: RONGXING LU, SENIOR MEMBER, IEEE

Year: 2019

Fog-enhanced Internet of Things (IoT) has gotten a lot of interest in recent years, because fog devices deployed at the network edge can increase IoT application performance while also improving security and privacy. In this research, we introduce a new Fog-enhanced IoT range query strategy that is both communication-efficient and privacy-preserving. The proposed system uses the BGN homomorphic encryption technique to protect both the query range and the data of individual IoT devices. In addition, the suggested system reorganises the range query using a range query expression, decomposition, and composition technique, which achieves $O(n)$ communication efficiency. The proposed system is indeed a privacy-preserving range query scheme, according to a thorough security analysis. Extensive tests show that the suggested approach is also efficient in terms of low range query generation cost and minimal communication overhead.

2.6 Assured Data Deletion with Fine-grained Access Control for Fog- based Industrial Applications

Author name: YONG YU, LIANG XUE, YANNAN LI, XIAOJIANG DU, MOHSEN GUIZANI AND BO YANG.

Year: 2018

Cloud computing, fog computing, and the Internet of Things (IoT) have made industries more affluent than they have ever been. By successfully integrating cloud computing, fog computing, and IoT infrastructure, a wide range of industrial systems, such as transportation and manufacturing systems, have been built. However, security and privacy considerations are important concerns in this sophisticated system, preventing wider implementation of these revolutionary techniques. We focus on ensured data deletion in this work, a topic that is vital but receives little attention in academia and industry. To begin, we present a framework for combining the cloud, fog, and things to handle data from industries or individuals. In this framework, we then focus on secure data deletion by presenting a guaranteed data deletion technique that satisfies both verified data deletion and flexible access control over sensitive data. When it comes to erasing cloud data and certifying its erasure, only data owners and fog devices are involved, which makes

11

the protocol viable due to its low latency and real-time interaction with fog. The suggested protocol makes use of attribute-based encryption, which can be proven to be secure using a standard model. Theoretical analysis reveals that our solution meets performance and functionality requirements, while implementation findings show that it is feasible.

2.7 Privacy-Preserving Image Retrieval and Sharing in Social Multimedia Applications

Author name: ZONGYE ZHANG , FUCAI ZHOU , SHIYUE QIN , QIANG JIA , AND ZIFENG XU

Year: 2020

Every day, millions of photos are generated through social multimedia applications. Because the public cloud has enormous storage capabilities, it is an ideal alternative for handling such a large number of photographs. Because photographs often contain a lot of sensitive information, social service providers must not only provide services like retrieval and sharing, but also ensure that the images' privacy is protected. In this research, we offer a system for content-based image retrieval and sharing in social multimedia applications that preserves anonymity. To produce image profile vectors, users first extract visual features from the photos and conduct locality-sensitive hashing methods on those features. The retrieval on the images is then modelled as an equality search on the image profile vectors. We create a secure index structure based on cuckoo hashing, which has a constant lookup time, to enable accurate and efficient retrieval. We've added picture insertion and deletion to our service to satisfy the needs of dynamic image updating. We process keys utilising secret sharing approaches to enable individuals holding similar photos to query and decrypt images independently, reducing key management and access control cost in social applications. Finally, we put the suggested scheme's prototype into action and conduct tests on encrypted image databases.

2.8 Scrubbing-aware Secure Deletion for 3D NAND Flash

Author name: WEI-CHEN WANG, CHIEN-CHUNG HO, MEMBER, IEEE, YUAN-HAO CHANG, SENIOR MEMBER, IEEE, TEI-WEI KUO, FELLOW, IEEE, AND PING-HSIEN LIN

Year: 2018

Unlike previous research, this project attempts to investigate a scrubbing-aware secure deletion architecture in order to improve the efficiency of secure deletion by utilising disturbance features. By arranging sensitive data to establish scrubbing-friendly patterns and using the proposed evaluation equations for each safe deletion command, the proposed approach could reduce secure deletion/scrubbing overheads. A number of experiments are used to assess the capability of our suggested design, and the findings are quite promising. The simulation findings demonstrate that the proposed design might reduce the average response time of each safe deletion instruction by 82 percent in a 128 Gbits 3D NAND flash memory device.

2.9 SUMMARY

This chapter had given the description about the literature survey for various techniques involved in Permanent data deletion in cloud.

SYSTEM STUDY

CHAPTER 3
SYSTEM STUDY

3.1 OVERVIEW

In this chapter, overview of existing system and proposed system for permanent data deletion are discussed.

3.2 EXISTING SYSTEM

The AES algorithm (also known as the Rijndael algorithm) is a symmetrical block cipher algorithm that takes plain text in blocks of 128 bits and converts them to cipher text using keys of 128, 192, and 256 bits. Since the AES algorithm is considered secure, it is in the worldwide standard. It uses a substitution permutation, or SP network, with multiple rounds to produce cipher text. The number of rounds depends on the key size being used. A 128-bit key size dictates ten rounds, a 192-bit key size dictates 12 rounds, and a 256-bit key size has 14 rounds. Each of these rounds requires a round key, but since only one key is inputted into the algorithm.

1. Key Generation - A key schedule algorithm is used to calculate all the round keys from the key. So the initial

key is used to create many different keys which will be used in the corresponding round of the encryption.

2. Encryption - Each round comprises of 4 steps. Sub Bytes, shift rows, Mix columns, Add round key. The Sub bytes does the substitution and Shift Rows and Mix Columns performs the permutation in the algorithm. Sub bytes implements the substitution. In this Sub bytes as the name implements each byte is substituted by another byte. This can be achieved by using a look up table called S-box. This substitution is done in a wat that a byte is never substituted by itself and also not substituted by another byte which is a compliment of the current byte. Shift Rows is just as its sounds. Each row is shifted a particular number of time. The first row is not shifted and the second row is shifted once to the left also the third row is shifted twice to the left. Mix Columns is basically a matrix multiplication with a specific matrix and thus the position of each byte in the column is changed as a result. This step is skipped in the last round. Now the resultant output of the previous stage is XOR-ed with the corresponding round key. Here the 16 bytes is not considered as a grid but just as 128 bytes of data. After all these rounds 128 bits of encrypted data is given back as output. This process is repeated until all the data to be encrypted undergoes this process.

3.Decryption - The stages in the rounds can be easily undone as these stages have been opposite to it which when performed reverts the changes. Each 128 blocks go through the 10,12 or 14 rounds, depending on the key size. The stages of decryption include Add round key, Inverse Mix Columns, Shift Rows, Inverse Sub Bytes. Here the decryption process is the reverse of encryption. Using AES algorithm encryption and decryption access and performance has been increased compared to RSA. Also while using RSA data has been outsourced to a webhost. Here, data has been encrypted and outsourced to cloud. Initially a virtual system has been created for working. In that virtual system environment, the input data(text) has been encrypted and saved as a chipper text in encrypted data file. Initially all files are empty as no process has been yet started. The encryption process has been started with a public key which has been generated with 128 bytes. As AES uses round algorithm the key generation process uses 128 bytes and take 10 rounds to produce public key and private key. Using the generated public key encryption has been done and the access has been provided for the encrypted data which has now converted to chipper text. The data has been decrypted when need of it. The process has been done more securely. The decrypted data has been deleted when it becomes unwanted for the data owners. The unwanted sensitive data that has been outsourced to the cloud also been deleted. So the data owners feels more secure that their privacy has been kept maintained.

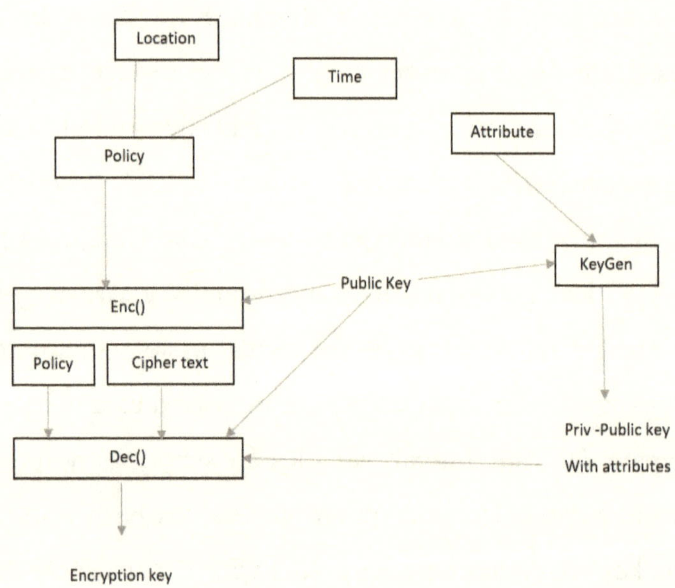

Figure 3.1 Schematic diagram of existing system

3.3 PROPOSED SYSTEM:

The suggested device employs AES to upload, encrypt, decrypt and delete the data from cloud. AES performs operations on bytes of data rather than in bits. Consider a scenario where a text has to be encrypted and deleted. Create a EC2 (There are many types of virtual machines like light sail etc.) virtual machine in amazon web services. Create instances on that virtual machine for running the code. On connecting to the cloud, there opens an inbuilt terminal. Say python3 has been used to write the code. Initially we will have the encrypted and the decrypted empty. On running the program file, user id and password needs to be entered in order to keep it secured. On entering the user name and password options are given like, to encrypt or to decrypt or to delete. If encrypt is selected, then key is generated and along with the key the text gets encrypted and the encrypted text gets stored in a file encrypted_data.txt inside the encrypted folder. To delete that, run the code again and go for delete option. Immediately it asks for security code for deletion. It is very confidential and can be used only by the data owners. On the other hand, the data users can only encrypt, decrypt and view the file. Only if the entered security key matches with the key that is exactly generated to be deleted, deletion process takes place. In the deletion process, we give the path to be deleted (i.e. the file in the encrypted and decrypted folder). The directory is given as a path. Remove method is used to delete the files named encrypted_data.txt and decrypted_data.txt. Now after deletion the original text along with the encrypted and the decrypted text gets deleted. It can never be retrieved once after deletion. If the security code given is wrong, then the message "Data not deleted" is displayed in the console.

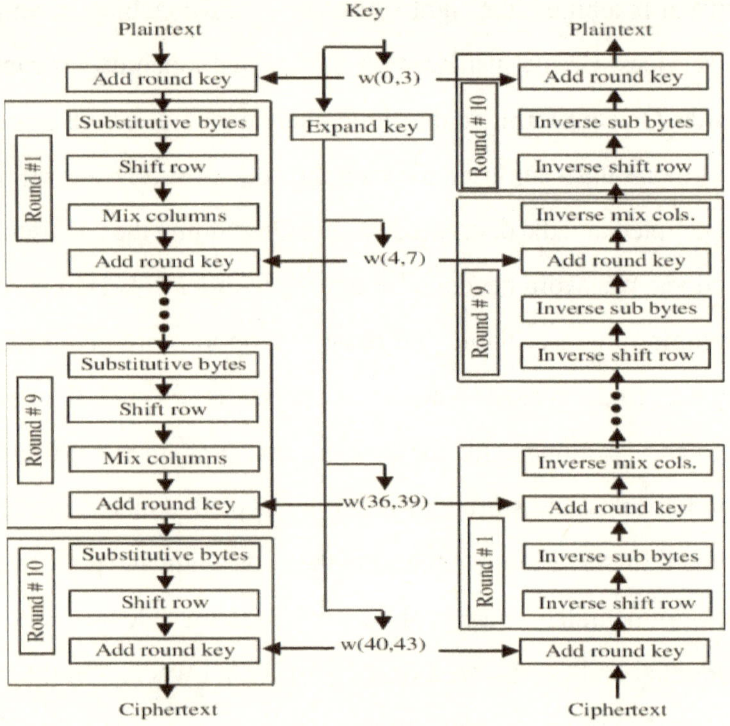

Figure 3.2 Schematic diagram of proposed system

3.4 SUMMARY

This chapter had described about the overview, comparison between the existing and proposed system for permanent data deletion in cloud.

SYSTEM DESIGN

CHAPTER 4
SYSTEM DESIGN

4.1 OVERVIEW

In this chapter system architectural design as well as the modules involved in the proposed system are discussed.

4.2 SYSTEM ARCHITECTURAL DESIGN

The architectural design for permanent data deletion in cloud is shown in Figure 4.1

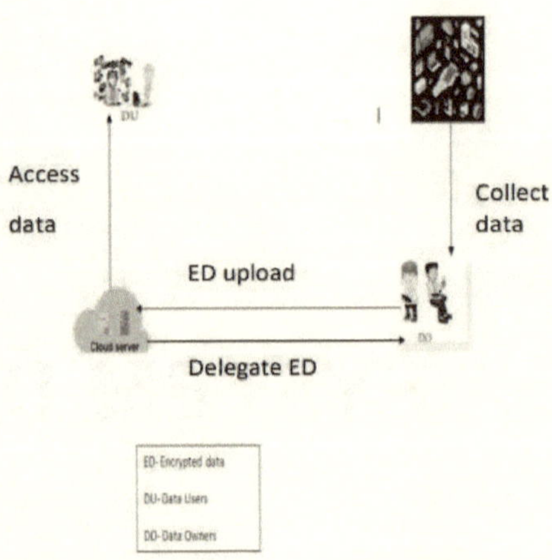

Figure 4.1 Architectural design for Permanent data deletion in cloud.

This system follows a systematic architecture design, and this diagram shows the complete architecture of the proposed system. There are many modules in the above diagram and each one is explained further.

4.3 MODULES DESCRIPTION

There are three major modules in the system each one performing a unique job and they are:

1. System Initialization

2. Data Upload

3. Data Encryption

4. Data Decryption

5. Data Deletion

4.3.1   System Initialization:

The data owners will gather information and assign tags to the obtained IoT data. Create the master key, public key, and secret key for encrypting and decrypting after defining tags.

4.3.2 Data Encryption:

It is the process of converting plain text data into an unreadable format, such as cipher text. The cipher text is generated using attribute-based encryption, and each cipher text is defined by a set of tags.

4.3.3 Data Decryption:

The encrypted data will be in a format that is unreadable by humans (cipher text). If the data user needs to see the file for whatever reason, he must first decrypt it so that the data user may see the original file.

4.3.4 Data Deletion:

The data owners create a deletion policy that specifies which cypher text should be removed. It removes the encryption that corresponds to the data owners' puncture policy. It cannot be decrypted using the secret key once it has been removed. When you delete a file, it not only deletes the encrypted and decrypted versions of the file, but it also deletes the original file.

4.3.5 Data Upload:

This procedure entails retrieving data or a file from the cloud and restoring it. This can be accomplished by typing the url into the postman site, which will cause the file to be posted to the cloud again for encryption, decryption, or deletion.

4.4 SUMMARY

In this chapter architectural designs as well as different kinds of modules in developing the proposed system were discussed with detailed explanation.

SYSTEM

IMPLEMENTATION

CHAPTER 5
SYSTEM IMPLEMENTATION

A detailed description of each of the different modules in the system design was provided in the previous chapter. As a continuation of that, this chapter will provide the implementation details pertaining to those modules.

5.1 IMPLEMENTATION OF AES ALGORITHM:

5.1.1 System initialisation:

Using AES algorithm creating and setting up the virtual machine is the system initialisation. Here the virtual machine is created in AWS cloud account and connecting to azure. Creating a virtual machine EC2 instance that directs to the terminal.

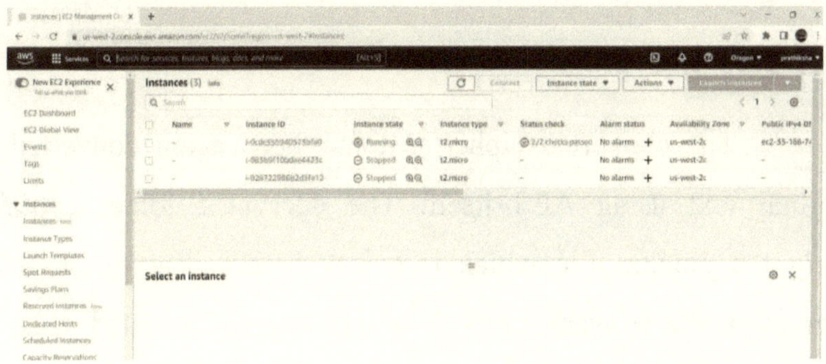

Figure 5.1.1 System Initialization for AES algorithm

5.1.2 Data encryption:

Initially the encrypted file will be empty whereas after giving input as string. It takes the input and converted cipher text and stored in encrypted folder in the encrypted_data.txt file. The given input has been converted into cipher text using AES. AES uses sp form that is substitution and permutation algorithm. It uses round key generation. The data (string) has been encrypted in the file as cipher text. The plain original text has been converted here.

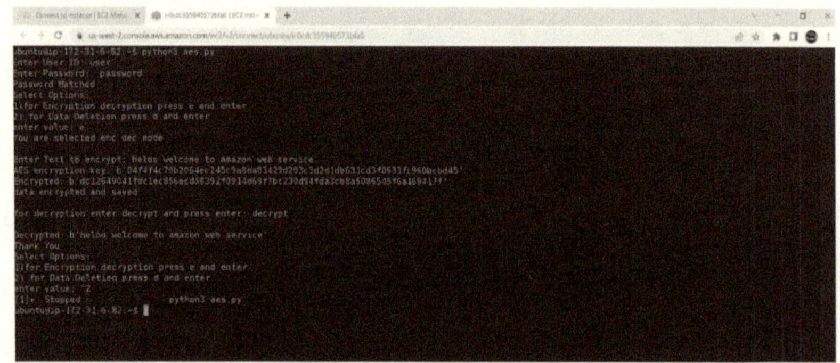

Figure 5.1.2 Data Encryption for AES algorithm

5.1.3 Data decryption:

The converted cipher text has been again converted to original text using AES itself. The decrypted folder contains decrypted_data.txt file which is empty before decryption. After decryption the converted cipher text has been converted again to original input and stored in the decrypted data .txt. The decrypted file contains the given input.

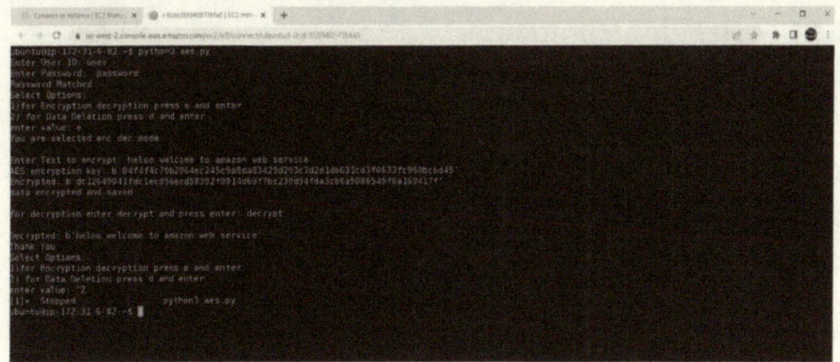

Figure 5.1.3 Data Decryption for AES algorithm

5.1.4 Data deletion:

The encrypted and decrypted text has been deleted using secret key which matches with the secret key provided by the data owners. Only the data owners know the secret key which has been kept privately for security. The data owners use the secret key and delete the encrypted and decrypted data. It removes the directory path and removes the file path from the virtual system.

Figure 5.1.4 Data Deletion for AES algorithm

5.2 IMPLEMENTATION OF HOMOMORPHIC ABE ALGORITHM:

5.2.1 System initialisation:

Here the system initialisation is setting up the virtual machine in the cloud. The virtual machine used for homomorphic ABE is light sail in AWS.

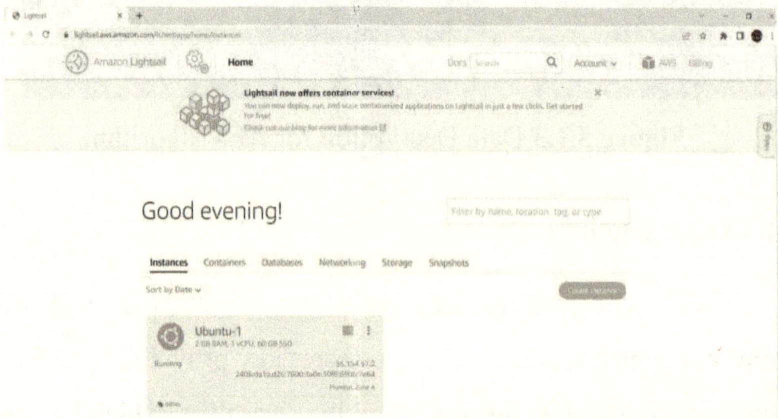

Figure 5.2.1 System Initialization for Homomorphic ABE algorithm

5.2.2 Data upload:

The input which is going to encrypted has been upload from the device through a site. The input has been upload and kept ready for encryption.

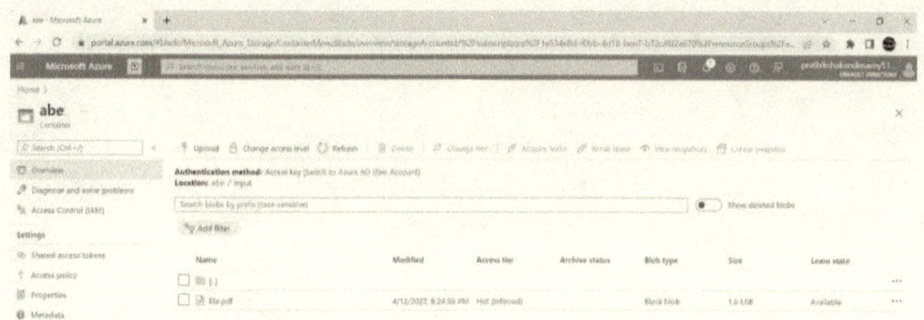

Figure 5.2.2 Data Upload for Homomorphic ABE algorithm

5.2.3 Data encryption:

We take Public key, and a message (M), along with an access structure for all the attributes (A). The output will be some cipher text (CT) and which embeds A, so that when a user satisfies the required attributes, they will be able to decrypt the cipher text. In this stage we take the master key (MK) and a number of attributes that define the key (S), and output a private key (SK). When we run the program the input has been provided for encryption. The public key private key has been generated. The input has been converted to cipher text and stored in a file. The input here given is pdf file and the whole pdf file has been converted to cipher text.

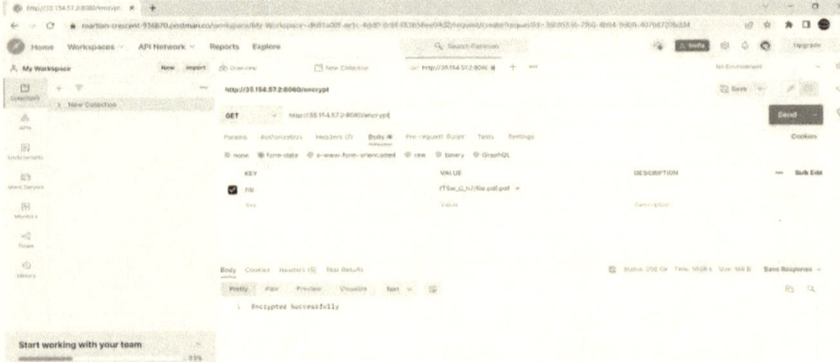

Figure 5.2.3 Data Encryption for Homomorphic ABE algorithm

5.2.4 Data decryption:

In this stage we take the public parameters (PK), the cipher text (CT—and which contains the access policy), and the secret key (for a given set of attributes S), and try to decrypt the cipher text. If successful we will get our message (M) back again. The encrypted data has been decrypted as given input file. It all takes in the cloud account and stored in a folder. The encryption and decryption runs and delivers the status in a website.

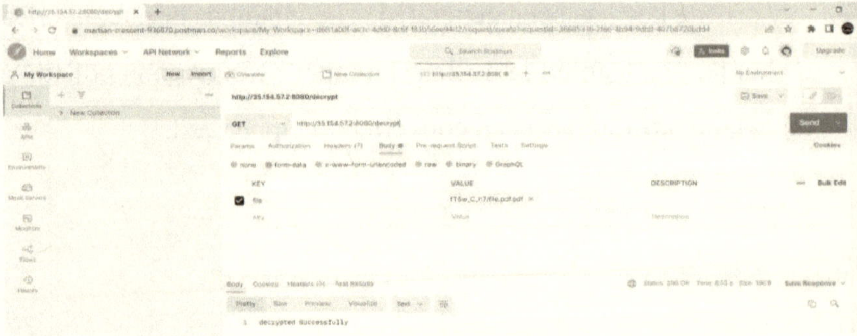

Figure 5.2.4 Data Decryption for Homomorphic ABE algorithm

5.2.5 Data deletion:

The data deletion is done by removing all the files. It includes the encrypted file and input data and decrypted file also it includes the generated public and private key.

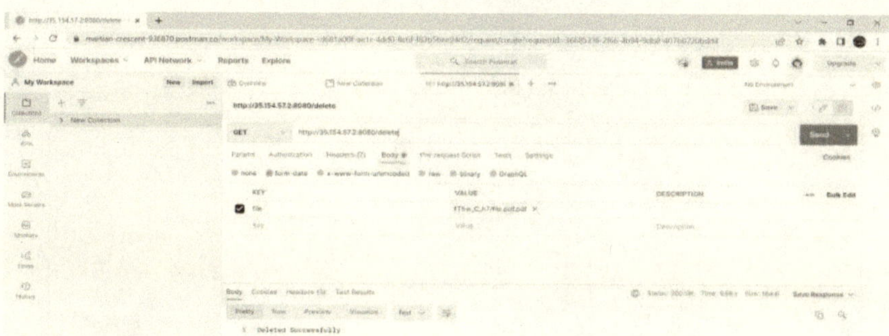

Figure 5.2.5 Data Deletion for Homomorphic ABE algorithm

5.3 SUMMARY

This chapter had given the brief description about the Literature survey, System Architectural design, Modules description. The next chapter deals with results and discussion.

RESULTS AND DISCUSSIONS

CHAPTER 6

RESULTS AND DISCUSSIONS

This chapter deals with the results that are obtained during the implementation.

6.1 IMPLEMENTATION AND RESULTS

IMPLEMENTATION RESULTS OF AES ALGORITHM

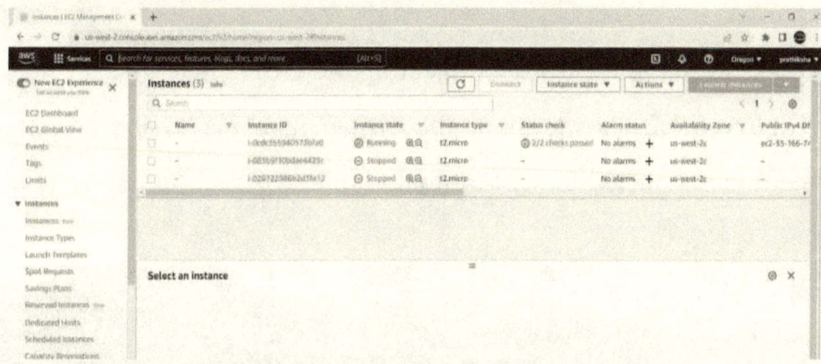

Figure 6.1.1 Creating the virtual machine

Figure 6.1.1 Creating an instance (virtual machine) in EC2. This is the part of system initialization. The virtual system started for connecting.

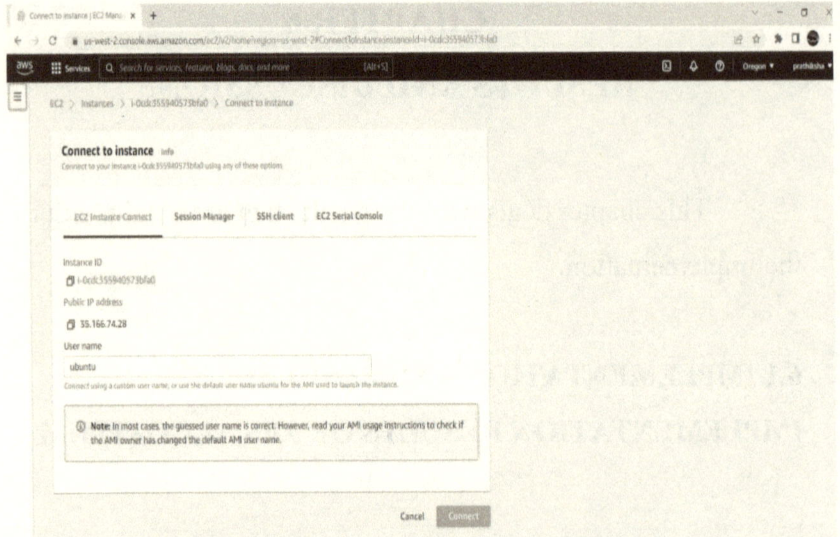

Figure 6.1.2 Connecting the virtual machine.

Figure 6.1.2 shows about the virtual machine to the cloud. It's getting connected to the terminal.

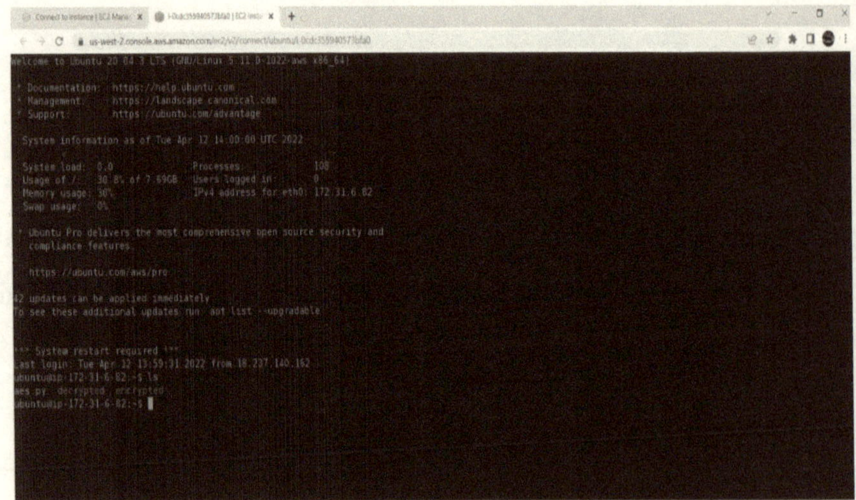

Figure 6.1.3 Viewing the files

Figure 6.1.3 describes about viewing the file in the local ssh terminal of the cloud.

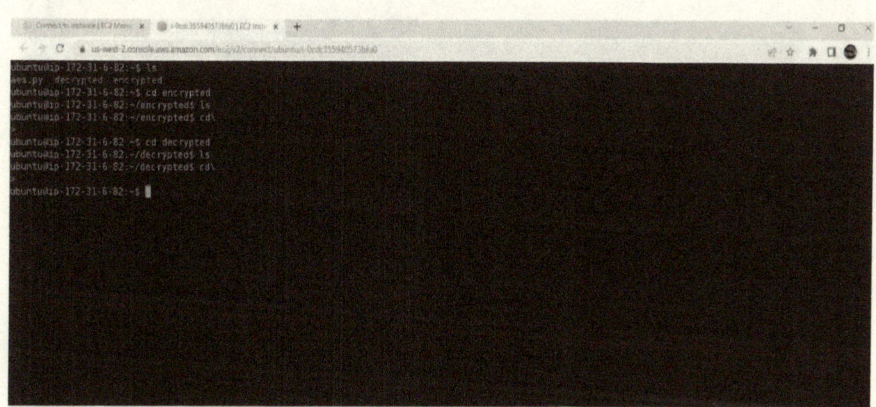

Figure 6.1.4 Empty encrypted and decrypted file

Figure 6.1.4 showing the initial stage of the folders in virtual system. Initially the encrypted and decrypted folders will be empty with no files inside.

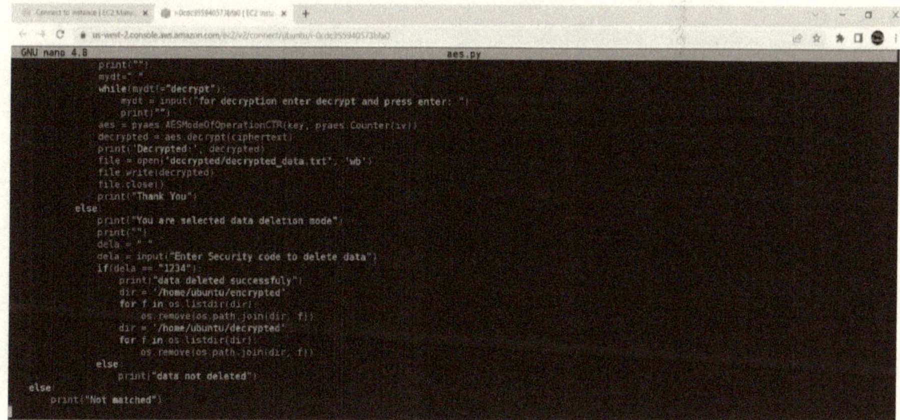

Figure 6.1.5 Code file

Figure 6.1.5 Viewing the code file with code inside (aes.py).

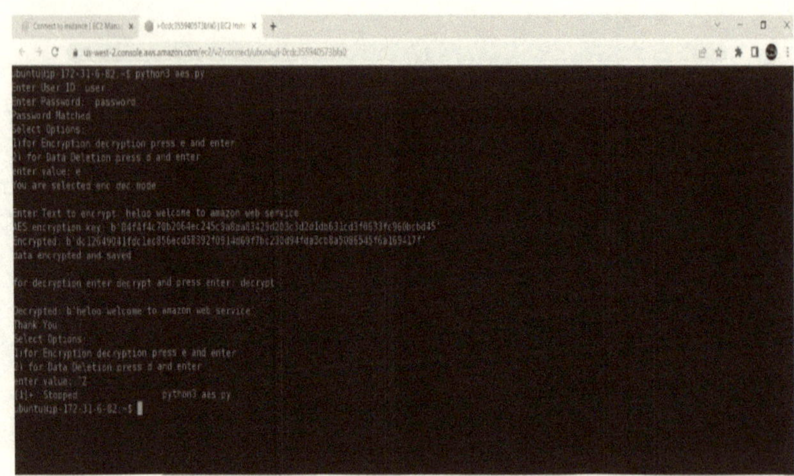

Figure 6.1.6 Running the code file, encrypting and decrypting it.

Figure 6.1.6 Run the code file aes.py and selecting the encryption option and then decryption option.

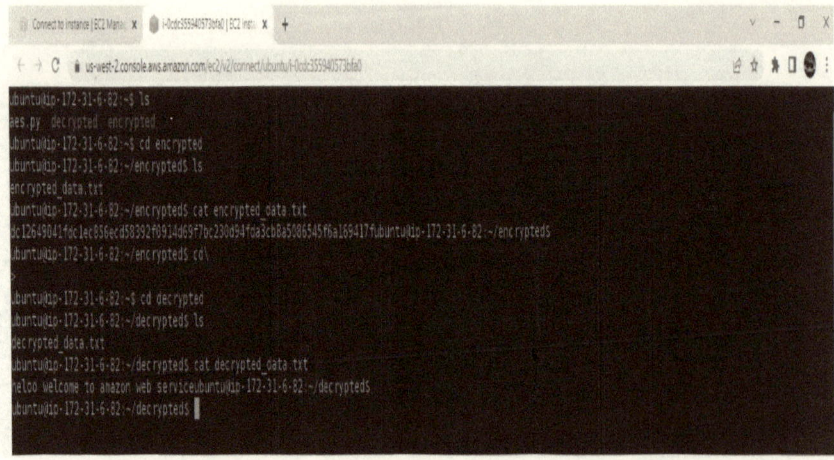

Figure 6.1.7 Encryption and Decryption folder

Figure 6.1.7 Viewing the encryption and decryption folder after encryption and decryption process.

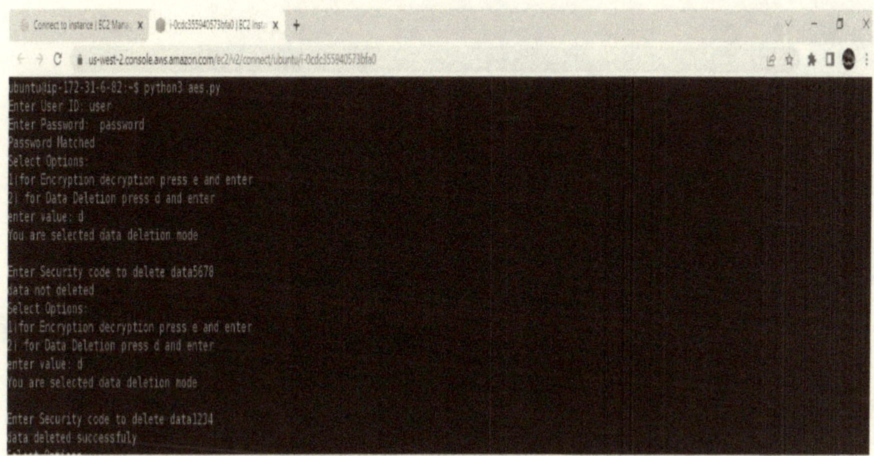

Figure 6.1.8 Deletion of data

Figure 6.1.8 Deleting the text by entering the correct security key.

Figure 6.1.9 After deletion

Figure 6.1.9 Viewing the encrypted and decrypted folder being empty after the deletion process.

IMPLEMENTATION RESULTS OF HOMOMORPHIC ABE ALGORITHM

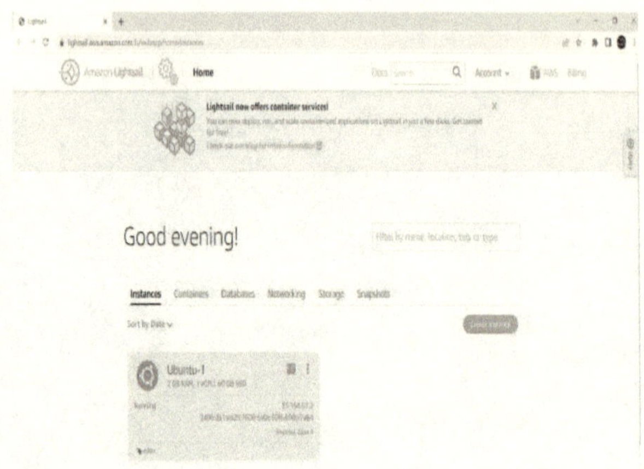

Figure 6.10 Creating virtual machine

Figure 6.10 Creating a light sail virtual machine in cloud. The initial stage of our process. Setting up the virtual machine for progress.

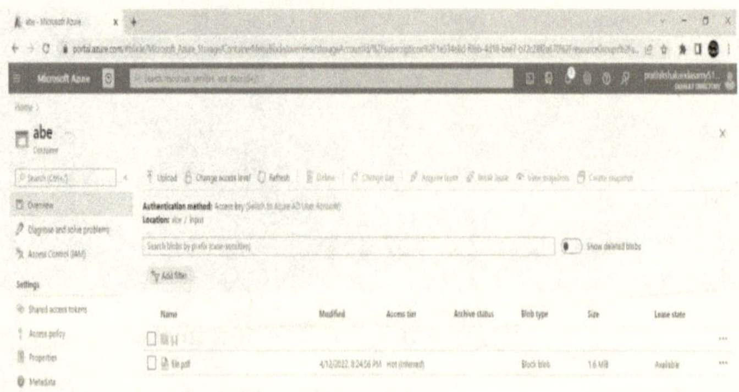

Figure 6.1.11 Upload the file

Figure 6.1.11 shows that uploading the file into the cloud by generating the link in the webhost.

Figure 6.1.12 Encryption

Figure 6.1.12 shows the encryption status and the downloaded encrypted file. The file viewing the cipher text.

```
pub_key - Notepad
File Edit Format View Help

 type a
q 8780710799663312522437781984754049815806883199414208211028653399266475630880022295707862517942266222142315585876958231745927771336731748132492512999 0224791
h 12016012264891146079388821366740534204802954401251311822919615131047207289359704531102844802183906537786776
r 730750818665451621361119245571504901405976559617
exp2 159
exp1 107
sign1 1
sign0 1
```

Figure 6.1.13 Viewing the master key, public key and private key generated during encryption.

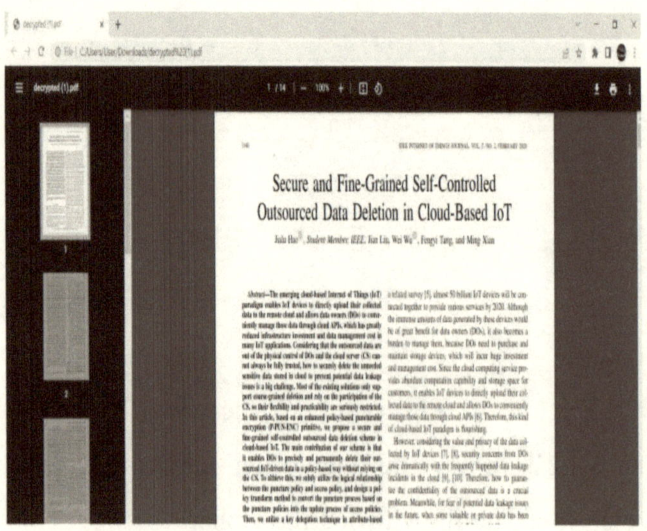

Figure 6.1.14 Decryption

Figure 6.1.14 Decrypting the file and viewing the cipher text.

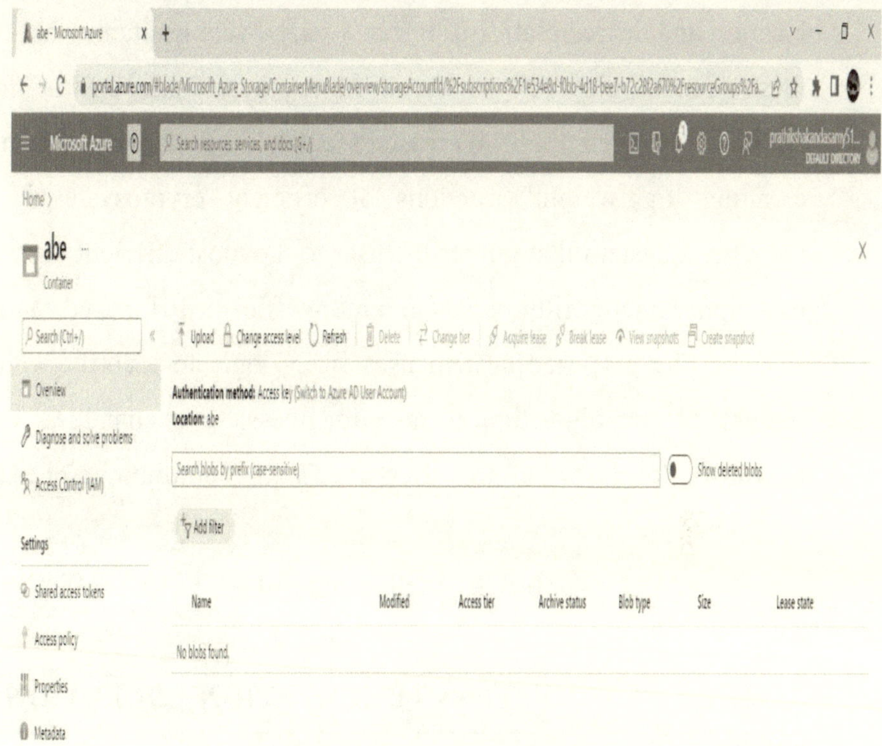

Figure 6.1.15 Deletion

Figure 6.1.15 Deleting the original, encrypted and decrypted folder. The complete deletion occurs here.

6.2 PERFORMANCE ANALYSIS

AES: The Internet of Things is progressively being used in almost every element of today's business. The ability to integrate online features with characteristics of the Internet of Things has resulted in better data management flexibility from virtually any location and device platform. Because users were hesitant to utilize these technologies due to the need to protect the information communicated, engineers increased security by encrypting data and creating "lightweight" versions of efficient cryptosystems. A judgement system that guides the user to the most efficient version of a ciphering algorithm leads to a more efficient IoT-based secure system. The proposed system uses fuzzy logic to identify which variant of the algorithm to use for message exchanges, with assurance levels to let the user choose the optimum ciphering technique.

Table 6.2.1 performance of AES using different input string

SIZE	ENCRYPTION	DECRYPTION	DELETION
8 bits	300µs	250 µs	100 µs
16 bits	310 µs	265 µs	108 µs
24 bits	315 µs	270 µs	115 µs

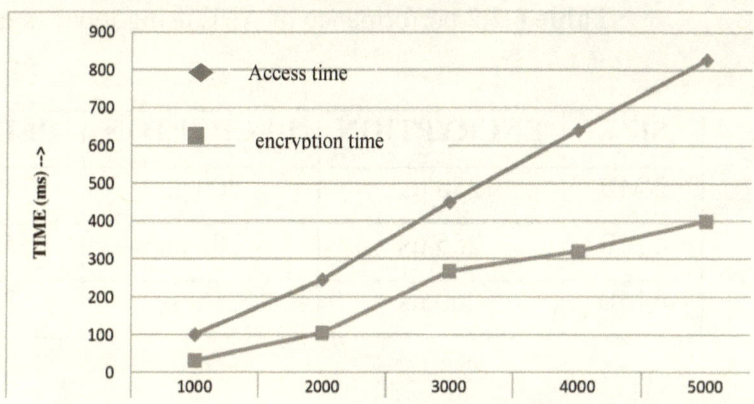

FIGURE 6.1 access time and encryption time of AES

ABE: In today's personalized and unique services and regulatory landscape, personal data privacy and security in cloud computing pose significant challenges. The attribute-based encryption (ABE)-based secure document self-destruction (ADS) technique suggested in this paper is a new combination of the ABE algorithm with a global-scale, decentralized distributed hash table (DHT) network. The ADS approach, in particular, can safeguard the privacy and security of old, archived sensitive data by ensuring that all copies of such documents are automatically destroyed after a user-specified period of time. According to the security and performance studies, the ADS strategy not only resists various hypothetical attacks, but also enables flexible access control policies for essential documents throughout their existence.

Table 6.2.2 performance of ABE using input as pdf

SIZE	ENCRYPTION	DECRYPTON	DELETION
2 MB	250 µs	200 µs	80 µs
4 MB	255 µs	205 µs	90 µs
6 MB	260 µs	215 µs	100 µs

This chapter had described the Implementation Results ad performance Analysis. The next chapter deals with Conclusion and Future Enhancement.

CONCLUSION AND FUTURE ENHANCEMENT

CHAPTER 7
CONCLUSION AND FUTURE ENHANCEMENT

7.1 CONCLUSION

This project focuses on permanently deleting data from the cloud such that it cannot be recovered or retrieved anywhere. Both AES and ABE algorithms were implemented using two mainstream cloud platforms. EC2 and light sail are two types of virtual machines that have been established. In terms of security, this method appears to outperform RSA and DES. AES has become the de facto global standard, and it is more secure than DES. Even in terms of time consumption, AES outperforms RSA.

7.2 FUTURE ENHANCEMENT

In future, this work can be further improved with the help of different algorithms for permanent data deletion in cloud with more security. This algorithm and enhanced form of this can benefit such areas where data should be deleted in order to effectively utilize the memory. The legacy system needed to be retired in order to be replaced with more recent and advanced technologies. In order to do so, data need to be deleted. These algorithms can highly be recommended for areas of such retirement activities.

REFERENCES

[1]. Jun Ma Minshen Wang, Jinbo Xiong, and Yongjin Hu **"CP-ABE-Based Secure and Verifiable Data Deletion in Cloud"** Volume 2021 |Article ID 8855341

[2]. Yassine EL Khanboubi, Mostafa Hanoune, Mohamed EI Ghazounai **"A New Data Deletion Scheme for a Block chain-based De-Duplication System in the cloud"**, Vol 13, No 2(2021)

[3]. Syed Ehtesham Ali, Kushboo Tackiar, P. Nitheesha, **"Secure Data Transmission and Deletion between Two Clouds without Overhead,"** 2021 JETIR May 2021, Volume 8, Issue 5.

[4]. Yuechi Tian1 & Tong Shao2 & Zhen Li1,2Yuechi Tian1 & Tong Shao2 & Zhen Li1,2, Published online: 6 January 2020

[5]. JimboXiang, LeiChen, Md Zakirul AlamBhuiyan, ChunjieCao, MinshenWang EntaoLuo, XimengLiu **"A secure data deletion scheme for IoT devices through key derivation encryption and data analysis"**, Volume 111, October 2020.

[6]. Wenfeng Zhang; Shiqi Jin, **"Research and Application of Data Privacy Protection Technology in Cloud Computing Environment Based on Attribute Encryption"** 2020 IEEE International Conference on Power, Intelligent Computing and Systems

[7]. Mustafa S. Abbas Suadad S. Mahdi Shahad A. Hussien **"Security Improvement of Cloud Data Using Hybrid Cryptography and Steganography"** 2020 International

Conference on Computer Science and Software Engineering (CSASE), Duos, Kurdistan Region – Iraq

[8]. S. Xu, G. Yang, Y. Mu, and X. Liu, **"A secure ICloud storage system with fifine-grained access control and decryption key exposure resistance,"** Future Generation Computer Systems, vol. 97, pp. 284–294, 2019.

[9]. S. Shanthi, R. J. Kannan, and S. Santhi, **"Efficient secure system of data in the cloud using steganography based cryptosystem with FSN,"** Mater. Today Proc., vol. 5, no. 1, pp. 1967–1973, 2018.

[10]. M. Thangavel; P. Varalakshmi; C. Abinaya, **"A Comparative Study of Attribute-Based Encryption Schemes for Secure Cloud Data Outsourcing"** 2017 Ninth International Conference on Advanced Computing (ICoAC)

[11]. V. Odelu, A. K. Das, M. K. Khan, K.-K. R. Choo, and M. Jo, **"Expressive CP-ABE scheme for mobile devices in IoT satisfying constant-size keys and cipher texts,"** IEEE Access, vol. 5, pp. 3273–3283, 2017.

[12]. Van-Hoan Hoang; Elyes Lehtihet; Yacine Ghamri-Doudane, **"Forward-Secure Data Outsourcing Based on Revocable Attribute-Based Encryption"** 2019 15th International Wireless Communications & Mobile Computing Conference (IWCMC)

[13]. M. D. Green and I. Miers, **"Forward secure asynchronous messaging from puncturable encryption,"** in Proc. IEEE Symp. Security Privacy (SP), 2015, pp. 305–320.

[14]. **Zhen Mo**; **Qingjun Xiao**; **Yian Zhou**; **Shigang Chen "On Deletion of Outsourced Data in Cloud Computing"** 04 December 2014.

[15]. J. Xiong et al., **"A secure data self-destructing scheme in cloud computing,"** IEEE Trans. Cloud Comput., vol. 2, no. 4, pp. 448–458, Oct.–Dec. 2014.

[16]. G. Wang, F. Yue, and Q. Liu, **"A secure self-destructing scheme for electronic data,"** J. Comput. Syst. Sci., vol. 79, no. 2, pp. 279–290, 2013.

[17]. R. Perlman, **"File system design with assured delete"**, in Proc. 3rd IEEE Int. Security Store. Workshop (SISW'05), 2005, 2017 Ninth International Conference on Advanced Computing (ICoAC)pp. 1–6.

[18]. Arthur Rahumed; Henry C.H. Chen; Yang Tang; Patrick P.C. Lee; John C.S. Lui **"A Secure Cloud Backup System with Assured Deletion and Version Control"**, 17 October 2011.

[19]. Yang Tang, Patrick P. C. Lee, John C. S. Luis†, and Radia Perlman FADE: **"Secure Overlay Cloud Storage with File Assured Deletion IEEE transactions dependable on secure computing"** vol:9 nos:6 years 2012.

[20]. J. Hao, J. Liu, W. Wu, F. Tang and M. Xian, **"Secure and Fine-Grained Self-Controlled Outsourced Data Deletion in Cloud-Based IoT,"** in IEEE Internet of Things Journal, vol. 7, no. 2, pp. 1140-1153, Feb. 2020

[21]. Jun Ma, Minshen Wang, Jinbo Xiong, Yongjin Hu, **"CP-ABE-Based Secure and Verifiable Data Deletion in Cloud"**, Security and Communication Networks, vol. 2021.

[22]. B. Sengupta, A. Dixit and S. Ruj, **"Secure Cloud Storage with Data Dynamics Using Secure Network Coding Techniques,"** in IEEE Transactions on Cloud Computing.

[23]. R. Lu, **"A New Communication-Efficient Privacy-Preserving Range Query Scheme in Fog-Enhanced IoT,"** in

IEEE Internet of Things Journal, vol. 6, no. 2, pp. 2497-2505, April 2019.

[24]. Y. Yu, L. Xue, Y. Li, X. Du, M. Guizani and B. Yang, **"Assured Data Deletion with Fine-Grained Access Control for Fog-Based Industrial Applications,"** in IEEE Transactions on Industrial Informatics, vol. 14, no. 10, pp. 4538-4547, Oct. 2018.

[25]. Z. Zhang, F. Zhou, S. Qin, Q. Jia and Z. Xu, **"Privacy-Preserving Image Retrieval and Sharing in Social Multimedia Applications,"** in IEEE Access, vol. 8, pp. 66828-66838, 2020.

[26]. W. -C. Wang, C. -C. Ho, Y. -H. Chang, T. -W. Kuo and P. -H. Lin, **"Scrubbing-Aware Secure Deletion for 3-D NAND Flash,"** in IEEE Transactions on Computer-Aided Design of Integrated Circuits and Systems, vol. 37, no. 11, pp. 2790-2801, Nov. 2018.